POETRY OF LAKELAND

POETRY OF LAKELAND
A Colour Souvenir in Verse

Compiled by
Ronald Sands

Front cover: Coniston Water and Coniston Old Man
Back cover: Loughrigg

ISBN 0 948511 00 1
Published by
Frank Peters Publishing Ltd
Kendal Cumbria
1985

First reprint 1989
Second reprint 1991

Printed by
Frank Peters (Printers) Ltd
Kendal, Cumbria

Photographs by
E A Bowness
M Gallagher
A Morris
R Mullin
T Parker

Foreword

The beauty of the Lake District is famous the world over and no other area of England has inspired so much poetry. Indeed many visitors seek out the Lake Country **because** they have first read about the region in poems and journals. Other visitors, overcome by the wonders of Lakeland, are naturally curious to learn how fellow pilgrims (and residents) have described their own experiences and reactions.

I hope both types of reader will find this anthology useful and enjoyable. The truly marvellous photographs have been chosen to augment the poetry and to stimulate you to visit the places described in the poems. This combination is also designed as a souvenir in the strict sense of the word — to help you relive your visits to the Lake District and, in Wordsworth's phrase, to recollect in tranquillity.

Readers will not be surprised to find that most, if not all, of the poems are celebratory and lyrical, expressive of the deep emotional power the Lake District often exerts on its admirers. There is, too, a strong sense of place.

I have allowed myself the luxury of including one poem which strictly belongs just outside the Lake District proper: Wordsworth's sonnet to the River Eden. Wordsworth spent most of his long life exploring the area, but only in his sixty-fourth year did he discover the quiet beauties of the Eden Valley. The poem serves as an urgent reminder to us all to seize every opportunity to experience the glories around us:—

"For things far off we toil, while many a good
Not sought, because too near, is never gained".

Happy Days!

Ronald Sands

Acknowledgements

Colin Baker and Donald Kelso of Frank Peters Ltd gave me invaluable help and encouragement in compiling this book; the inspired design by Ronnie Mullin is a testimony to his own enthusiasm for the project and we were much helped by the staff of the Cumbria Library Service at Carlisle and Kendal. The photographers represented in this volume have made a notable contribution, responding to the beauty of the Lakeland landscape and providing fitting illustrations to the poems. I am grateful most of all to the poets whose work appears in these pages: if they were alive today, I would like to think they would be pleased and proud of an anthology which will introduce their poems to a new generation of readers.

Contents

A Crosthwaite Belfry Song	H D Rawnsley	9
Not raised in nice proportions	William Wordsworth	11
The First Swallow	H D Rawnsley	12
The Holly Tree	Robert Southey	12
The Daffodils (I)	William Wordsworth	14
The Daffodils (II)	William Wordsworth	15
Calm Wastwater	Christopher North	17
Stormy Wastwater	Christopher North	17
Written in March	William Wordsworth	18
To the Cuckoo	William Wordsworth	19
Low Wood, Winandermere	Edward Quillinan	21
The River Brathay	F W Faber	21
A Flower of Fairfield	Edward Quillinan	22
The Wounded Lamb	F W Faber	23
Home from Italy	H D Rawnsley	23
On Grasmere Island	William Wordsworth	24
The Birch of Silver-How	Edward Quillinan	25
The Kirk of Ulpha	William Wordsworth	28
Afterthought	William Wordsworth	28
The Hayeswater Boat	Matthew Arnold	29
Yearning for the Lakes	John Ruskin	31
A Memory of Grasmere	Felicia Dorothea Hemans	33
Beside the Mountain Rill	Hartley Coleridge	34
Mountain Tarns	F W Faber	35
The Wanderer Returns	Robert Southey	36
The Tables Turned	William Wordsworth	37
Sunset over the Langdale Pikes	William Wordsworth	38
Blea Tarn House, Little Langdale	William Wordsworth	39
The Enchanted Castle of St John's Vale	Walter Scott	41
De Vaux Discovers the Castle of St John	Walter Scott	42
Descent of Skiddaw	John Ruskin	47
A Fell Walk	Matthew Arnold	48
Wytheburn Chapel and Inn	Hartley Coleridge	49
Castlerigg Stone Circle	John Keats	51
Thirlmere to Castlerigg	John Ruskin	52

The Knight's Tomb	Samuel Taylor Coleridge	53
Stern Blencartha	Samuel Taylor Coleridge	53
Savage Grandeur	John Dalton	54
The Cataract of Lodore	Robert Southey	55
Hellvellyn	Walter Scott	58
Fidelity	William Wordsworth	60
The Pass of Kirkstone	William Wordsworth	63
To a Rainbow	William Wordsworth	64
Airey Force Valley	William Wordsworth	64
Midnight Adoration	Christopher North	65
Foxgloves at Brandelhow	H D Rawnsley	67
Brougham Castle	William Wordsworth	68
To a Butterfly	William Wordsworth	70
Heather on Lonscale	H D Rawnsley	70
Yew Trees	William Wordsworth	71
Skating on Esthwaitewater	William Wordsworth	72
Skating on Derwentwater	H D Rawnsley	74
Fountains, Meadows, Hills, and Groves	William Wordsworth	74
Wordsworth Remembered	Matthew Arnold	75
The River Eden	William Wordsworth	76
A Shadow on Scafell	H D Rawnsley	76
Index of Poets		78
Index of First Lines		

A Crosthwaite Belfry Song

NEW YEAR'S DAY

Cheery Crosthwaite ringers, climb your belfry stair,
Set your carol-singers carolling in air;
    Loud mouth and soft mouth,
    Low mouth, aloft mouth,
    Let the eight bell voices
    Say the vale rejoices.
That another year has gone–has gone with all its care.

Set your ropes a-dancing at your captain's call,
Let the shadows glancing follow up the wall.
    'Single!' cry, 'Bob!' shout,
    In and out dodge about,
    Till the vale rejoices
    That the eight bell voices
    Tell a happy glad New Year has come for
    one and all.

    H D Rawnsley.

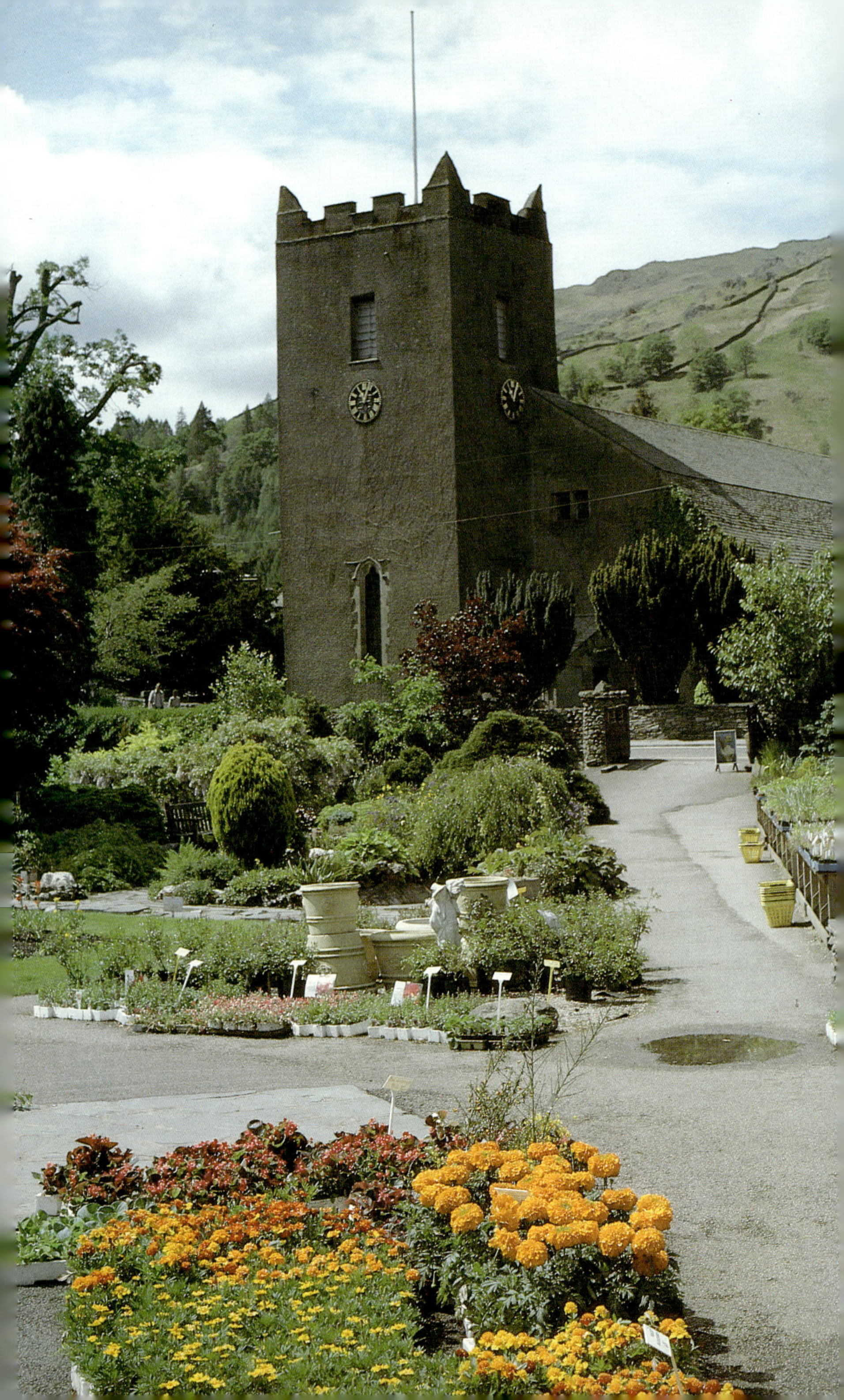

From "The Excursion"

Not raised in nice proportions was the Pile
But large and massy, for duration built,
With pillars crowded and the roof upheld
By naked rafters intricately crossed.

William Wordsworth

ST OSWALD'S CHURCH, GRASMERE: *parts of the present building date back to at least the 13th Century and its unique charm has much to do with the structural enlargements spread over several hundred years. Wordsworth planted eight yews in the churchyard, where he and his family are buried. The famous rushbearing ceremony is still observed on the Saturday nearest St Oswald's Day (5th August), a reminder of the time when the earthen floor of the church was strewn with rushes. In 1854 the lych-gate cottage ceased to be the school and became the home of Sarah Nelson who baked funeral cakes. Her traditional gingerbread is still sold there today.*

The First Swallow

I heard the wheat-ear singing in the dale,
    I saw the ouzel curtsey to the sun,
    And cried, 'The days of winter sure are done,
The spring upon the mountains doth prevail,
Soon shall the cuckoo come to tell her tale.'
    E'en as I spake where Calder's ripples run
    To seek the shining Solway, there came one
Songless but sweeter than the nightingale.

From silent wastes and those dumb Memphian hills
    Where dead men slumber in Sakkarah's dunes,
    He came, he could not speak our English tongue,
But as he flashed above the daffodils
    On bluest April air he wrote in runes
    That Love was near, and Life again was young.

    H. D. Rawnsley.

The Holly Tree

O Reader! hast thou ever stood to see
    The Holly Tree?
The eye that contemplates it well perceives
    Its glossy leaves
Order'd by an intelligence so wise,
As might confound the Atheist's sophistries.

Below, a circling fence, its leaves are seen
    Wrinkled and keen;
No grazing cattle through their prickly round
    Can reach to wound;
But as they grow where nothing is to fear,
Smooth and unarm'd the pointless leaves appear.

I love to view these things with curious eyes,
    And moralize:
And in this wisdom of the Holly Tree
    Can emblems see
Wherewith perchance to make a pleasant rhyme,
One which may profit in the after time.

Thus, though abroad perchance I might appear
    Harsh and austere,
To those who on my leisure would intrude
    Reserved and rude,
Gentle at home amid my friends I'd be
Like the high leaves upon the Holly Tree.

And should my youth, as youth is apt I know,
    Some harshness show,
All vain asperities I day by day
    Would wear away,
Till the smooth temper of my age should be
Like the high leaves upon the Holly Tree.

And as when all the summer trees are seen
    So bright and green,
The Holly leaves a sober hue display
    Less bright than they,
But when the bare and wintry woods we see,
What then so cheerful as the Holly Tree?

So serious should my youth appear among
    The thoughtless throng,
So would I seem amid the young and gay
    More grave than they,
That in my age as cheerful I might be
As the green winter of the Holly Tree.

    Robert Southey

The Daffodils (I)

I wandered lonely as a Cloud
That floats on high o'er Vales and Hills,
When all at once I saw a crowd,
A host of dancing daffodils;
Along the Lake, beneath the trees,
Ten thousand dancing in the breeze

The waves beside them danced, but they
Out did the sparkling waves in glee:—
A poet could not but be gay
In such a laughing company:
I gaz'd — and gaz'd — but little thought
What wealth to me the shew had brought:

For oft when on my couch I lie
In vacant or in pensive mood,
They flash upon that inward eye
Which is the bliss of solitude;
And then my heart with pleasure fills,
And dances with the daffodils.

William Wordsworth

Note: This is the original version of the famous poem, composed in 1804 and published in 1807. The final version opposite was published in 1815 with the addition of a new stanza. Other changes include substituting "golden" for "dancing" and "jocund" for "laughing".

DORA'S FIELD is adjacent to Rydal Church. Formerly known as the Rashfield, Wordsworth purchased the land in 1825 with the intention of building a house there. He later gave it to his daughter Dora. In the spring the splendid show of daffodils attracts many photographers. These daffodils however are not the ones which inspired Wordsworth's famous poem. "I wandered lonely as a cloud" is a description of a scene near Gowbarrow on the shores of Ullswater. The church contains a memorial window to the Victorian poet and educationist Matthew Arnold who lived nearby, at Fox How on the Under Loughrigg road.

The Daffodils (II)

I wandered lonely as a cloud
    That floats on high o'er vales and hills,
When all at once I saw a crowd,
    A host, of golden daffodils;
Beside the lake, beneath the trees,
Fluttering and dancing in the breeze.

Continuous as the stars that shine
    And twinkle on the milky way,
They stretched in never-ending line
    Along the margin of a bay:
Ten thousand saw I at a glance,
Tossing their heads in sprightly dance.

The waves beside them danced; but they
    Out-did the sparkling waves in glee:
A poet could not but be gay,
    In such a jocund company:
I gazed–and gazed–but little thought
What wealth the show to me had brought:

For oft, when on my couch I lie
    In vacant or in pensive mood,
They flash upon that inward eye
    Which is the bliss of solitude;
And then my heart with pleasure fills,
And dances with the daffodils.

    William Wordsworth.

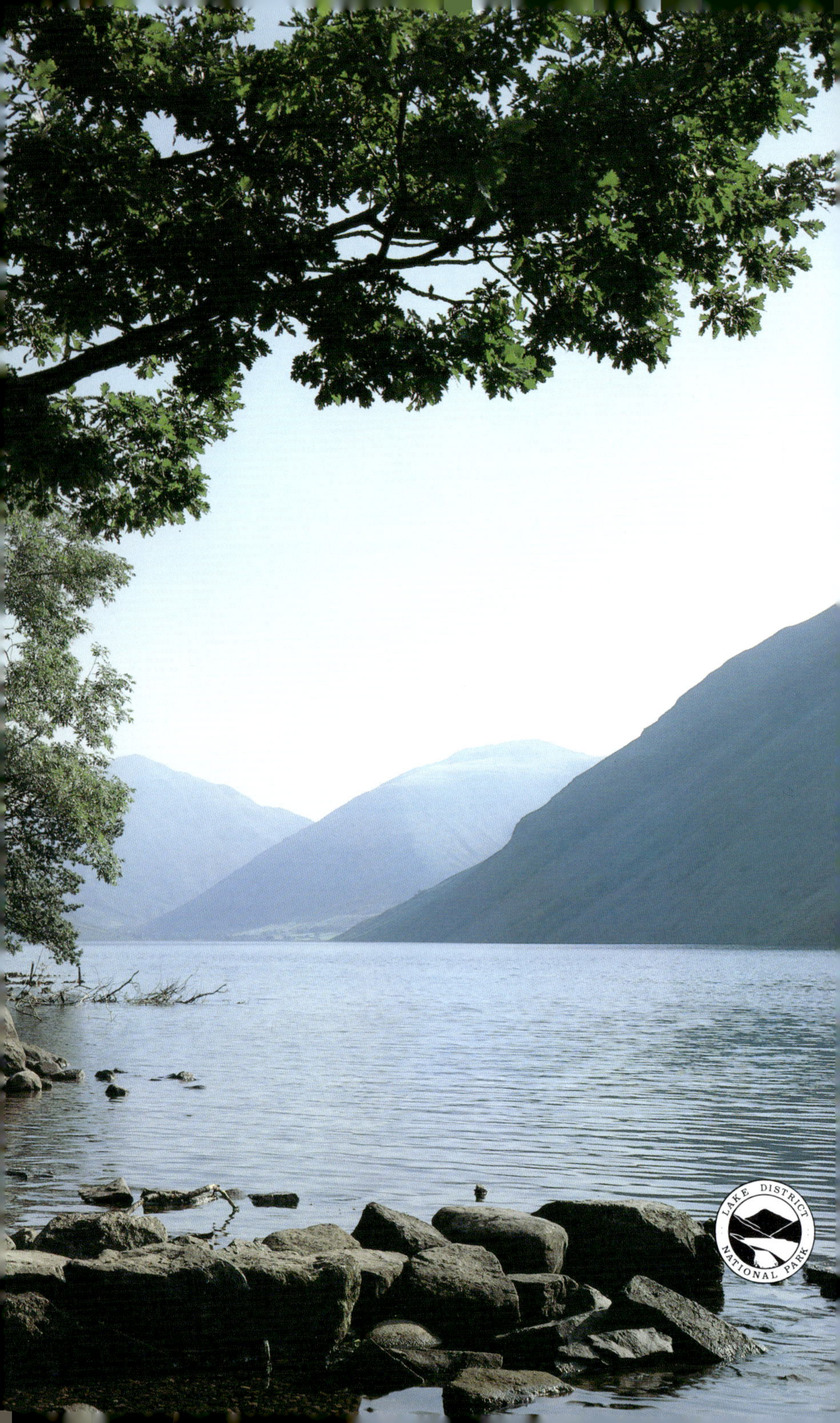
LAKE DISTRICT
NATIONAL PARK

Calm Wastwater

Is this the Lake, the cradle of the storms,
Where silence never tames the mountain-roar,
Where poets fear their self-created forms,
Or, sunk in trance severe, their God adore?
Is this the Lake, for ever dark and loud
With wave and tempest, cataract and cloud?
Wondrous, O Nature! is thy sovereign power,
That gives to horror hours of peaceful mirth;
For here might beauty build her summer-bower!
Lo! Where yon rainbow spans the smiling earth,
And, clothed in glory, through a silent shower
The mighty sun comes forth, a godlike birth;
While, neath his loving eye, the gentle Lake
Lies like a sleeping child too blest to wake.

Stormy Wastwater

There is a Lake hid far among the hills,
That raves around the throne of solitude,
Not fed by gentle streams, or playful rills,
But headlong cataract and rushing flood.
There, gleam no lovely hues of hanging wood,
No spot of sunshine lights her sullen side;
For horror shaped the wild in wrathful mood,
And o'er the tempest heaved the mountains' pride.
If thou art one, in dark presumption blind,
Who vainly deems't no spirit like to thine,
That lofty genius deifies thy mind,
Fall prostrate here at Nature's stormy shrine,
And as the thunderous scene disturbs thy heart
Lift thy changed eye, and own how low thou art.

   Christopher North.

WASTWATER is England's deepest lake, in parts being well below sea level. This classic view provided the basis for the Lake District National Park emblem. The shapely summit in the centre is Great Gable with Yewbarrow to the left and Lingmell to the right. At 11.00am on the Sunday nearest to the 11th November there is an annual Rememberance Service held on the summit to commemorate the walkers and climbers who have died in war. The quickest ascent is from the road summit of Honister Pass. In the churchyard at Wasdale Head are memorials of a different kind — poignant gravestones of climbers who have come to grief on the demanding rock faces of the surrounding hills.

Written in March

WHILE RESTING ON THE BRIDGE AT
THE FOOT OF BROTHER'S WATER

    The Cock is crowing,
    The stream is flowing,
    The small birds twitter,
    The lake doth glitter,
The green field sleeps in the sun;
    The oldest and youngest
    Are at work with the strongest;
    The cattle are grazing,
    Their heads never raising;
There are forty feeding like one!

    Like an army defeated
    The snow hath retreated,
    And now doth fare ill
    On the top of the bare hill;
The Ploughboy is whooping-anon-anon:
    There's joy in the mountains;
    There's life in the fountains;
    Small clouds are sailing,
    Blue sky prevailing;
The rain is over and gone!

    William Wordsworth.

To the Cuckoo

O blithe New-comer! I have heard,
I hear thee and rejoice.
O Cuckoo! shall I call thee Bird,
Or but a wandering Voice?

While I am lying on the grass
Thy twofold shout I hear;
From hill to hill it seems to pass
At once far off, and near.

Though babbling only to the Vale,
Of sunshine and of flowers,
Thou bringest unto me a tale
Of visionary hours.

Thrice welcome, darling of the Spring!
Even yet thou art to me
No bird, but an invisible thing,
A voice, a mystery;

The same whom in my schoolboy days
I listened to; that Cry
Which made me look a thousand ways
In bush, and tree, and sky.

To seek thee did I often rove
Through woods and on the green;
And thou wert still a hope, a love;
Still longed for, never seen.

And I can listen to thee yet;
Can lie upon the plain
And listen, till I do beget
That golden time again.

O blessèd Bird! the earth we pace
Again appears to be
An unsubstantial, faery place;
That is fit home for Thee!

    William Wordsworth

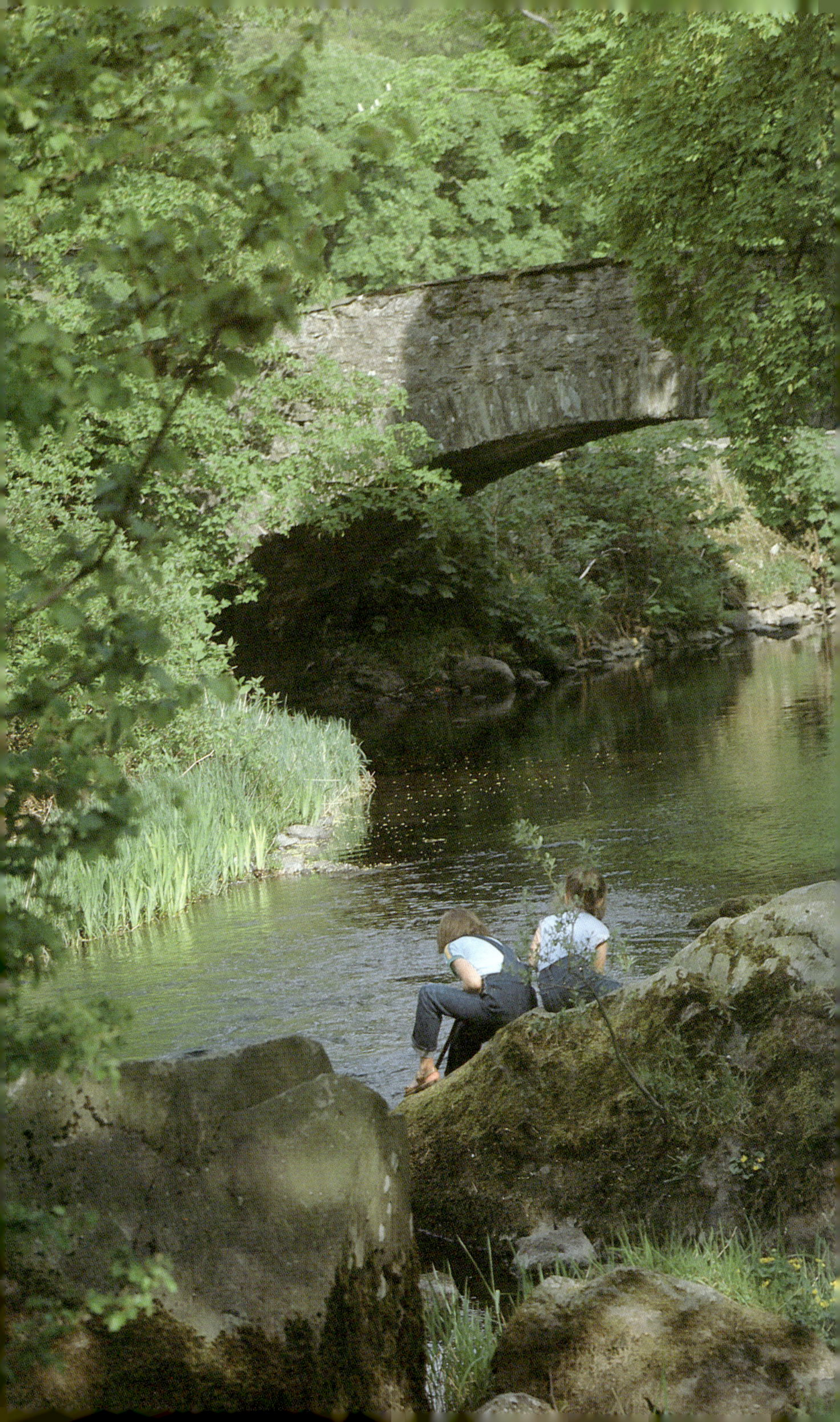

Low Wood, Winandermere

In such a scene, on such a day,
I crown'd my bride the queen of May
    With wreath by Erin's daughters braided;
The hills were grand, the bowers were gay,
    Roughly bold, and softly shaded;
The lake was calm, and bright, and clear,
Like the lake of Windermere.

Years since have passed of joy and pain,
I've never heard her voice complain,
    In sickness and in sadness;
In health I've never known her vain,
    Nor arrogant in gladness.
Would that I now her voice could hear
By the lake of Windermere.

    Edward Quillinan (MAY 1, 1824)

The River Brathay

Low spirits are a sin,–a penance given
To over-talking and unthoughtful mirth.
There is nor high nor low in holiest heaven,
Nor yet in hearts where heaven hath hallowed earth.
Still there are some whose growth is won in strife,
And who can bear hot suns through all their life:
But rather for myself would I forego
High tides of feeling and brief moods of power,
Than share those languors with the showy flower,
Which the shade-loving herb doth never know.
O Brathay! wisely in thy winter grounds,
Wisely and sweetly are thy currents chiming,
Thus happily to every season timing
The same low waters and the same low sounds.

    F. W. Faber

PELTER BRIDGE spans the River Rothay at Rydal and is a favourite starting point for the popular walk along the "quiet" side of Rydalwater. From this path the whitewashed Nab Cottage can be seen across the lake: De Quincey and later Hartley Coleridge lodged here. The River Rothay, fed by mountain becks which have their sources above Dunmail, flows through Grasmere and Rydalwater before joining the River Brathay at the northern end of Windermere.

A Flower of Fairfield

As once I roam'd the fells, to brood,
In silence and in solitude,
   On fancies all my own,
In one of Nature's hiding spots
I found a flower as shy as thoughts
   That love to be alone;

A primrose in a nook enshrined;
A rocky cleft with mosses lined,
   And over-arch'd with fern;
And guarded well from wandering hoof,
By two rough sentries arm'd in proof,-
   A bramble and a thorn.

Wrens hide not in more jealous cells
Their precious hoard of speckled shells,
   Than that where hidden blew
This golden treasure of the Spring,
As brightly delicate a thing
   As ever Eden knew.

This is the very type, said I,
Of yon fair nymph, so lone and shy,
   Whose spirit charms the wild!
And hither from her laurell'd nook,
Of this her floral self to look,
   I led the Poet's Child.

Together on the vernal gem,
That seem'd to tremble to its stem
   With trouble not its own,
We gazed as silent as the flower;
But never from that happy hour
   My heart has been alone.

   Edward Quillinan

The Wounded Lamb

I saw a shepherd with a wounded lamb,
Which he had found in pain and almost dead
Among the blue stones upon Rydal Head,
Where, plaintive tenant of the moor, the dam
With sorrow in her large round eyes was left,
Of that white, gleaming creature now bereft.
The village children gathered in a ring,
Doubtful, as round some disenchanted spell:
For three days they had seen it wandering
A bodily sunbeam on the rocky fell.
It puzzles them to think that on the morrow
That patch of light will not be up on high;
Yet do they love it more, for common sorrow
Begets in wonder's stead sweet sympathy.

    F.W. Faber

Home from Italy

There are no snow-white oxen in the dales
    To drag with rolling gait the narrow wain;
    No cypress plumes the hill, and in the plain
I scent no vines, I hear no nightingales;
But the same rose, whose beauty there prevails,
    Shuts her pink petals from the gentle rain;
    The same swifts cry above the topmost vane,
And high in air the self-same buzzard sails.

Thro' silent sunburnt flats no Tiber streams,
    No Amiata shines divinely blue,
      No purple city dreams about its dome;
But Skiddaw lifts his bulk of changeful hue,
Thro' lush green meads the Greta sounds and gleams,
    And one fair garden calls the wanderer home.

    H.D. Rawnsley

On Grasmere Island

WRITTEN WITH A PENCIL UPON A STONE IN THE WALL OF THE HOUSE (AN OUTHOUSE), ON THE ISLAND AT GRASMERE

Rude is this Edifice, and Thou has seen
Buildings, albeit rude, that have maintained
Proportions more harmonious and approached
To closer fellowship with ideal grace.
But take it in good part:–alas! the poor
Vitruvius of our village had no help
From the great City; never, upon leaves
Of red Morocco folio saw displayed,
In long succession, pre-existing ghosts
Of Beauties yet unborn–the rustic Lodge
Antique, and Cottage with verandah graced,
Nor lacking, for fit company, alcove,
Green-house, shell-grot, and moss-lined hermitage.
Thou see'st a homely Pile, yet to these walls
The heifer comes in the snow-storm and here
The new-dropped lamb finds shelter from the wind.
And hither does one Poet sometimes row
His pinnace, a small vagrant barge, up-piled
With plenteous store of heath and withered fern,
(A lading which he with his sickle cuts,
Among the mountains) and beneath this roof
He makes his summer couch, and here at noon
Spreads out his limbs, while, yet unshorn, the Sheep,
Panting beneath the burden of their wool,
Lie round him, even as if they were a part
Of his own Household: nor, while from his bed
He looks, through the open door-place, toward the lake
And to the stirring breezes, does he want
Creations lovely as the work of sleep–
Fair sights, and visions of romantic joy!

    William Wordsworth

The Birch of Silver-How

I'll doubt no more that Fairies dwell
    At least in one enchanted place,
Though wisdom long since rang the knell
    Of Oberon and all his race:
        They haunt Kehlbarrow's woody brow,
        Amid the rocks of Silver-How!

And if you climb beyond the wood
    You'll there a Fairy chapel see;
And there, in spite of wind and flood,
    Beside it find a goodly tree:
        Of upright stem and flexile bough,
        The Fairy-tree of Silver How.

. . .

The red-breast that was wont to sing
    His matins on its topmost spray,
Now wheel'd aloof his fickle wing
    To chaunt elsewhere his roundelay:
        To thriving trees his court he paid,
        So well he knew the poet's trade.

The sun went down, but when again
    He rose and look'd on Silver-How,
The red-breast trill'd his morning strain
    Upon his old accustom'd bough:
        For lo! the tree that prostrate lay,
        Erectly stood in face of day.

It rose, untouch'd by human hands,
And now a living wonder stands
    On that enchanted fell!
Wise sceptic, you deny in vain
To wild kehlbarrow's fairy fane
    A priestess and a spell:
Go profit by my elfin creed,
And lift the fallen in their need
    As secretly and well!

    Edward Quillinan

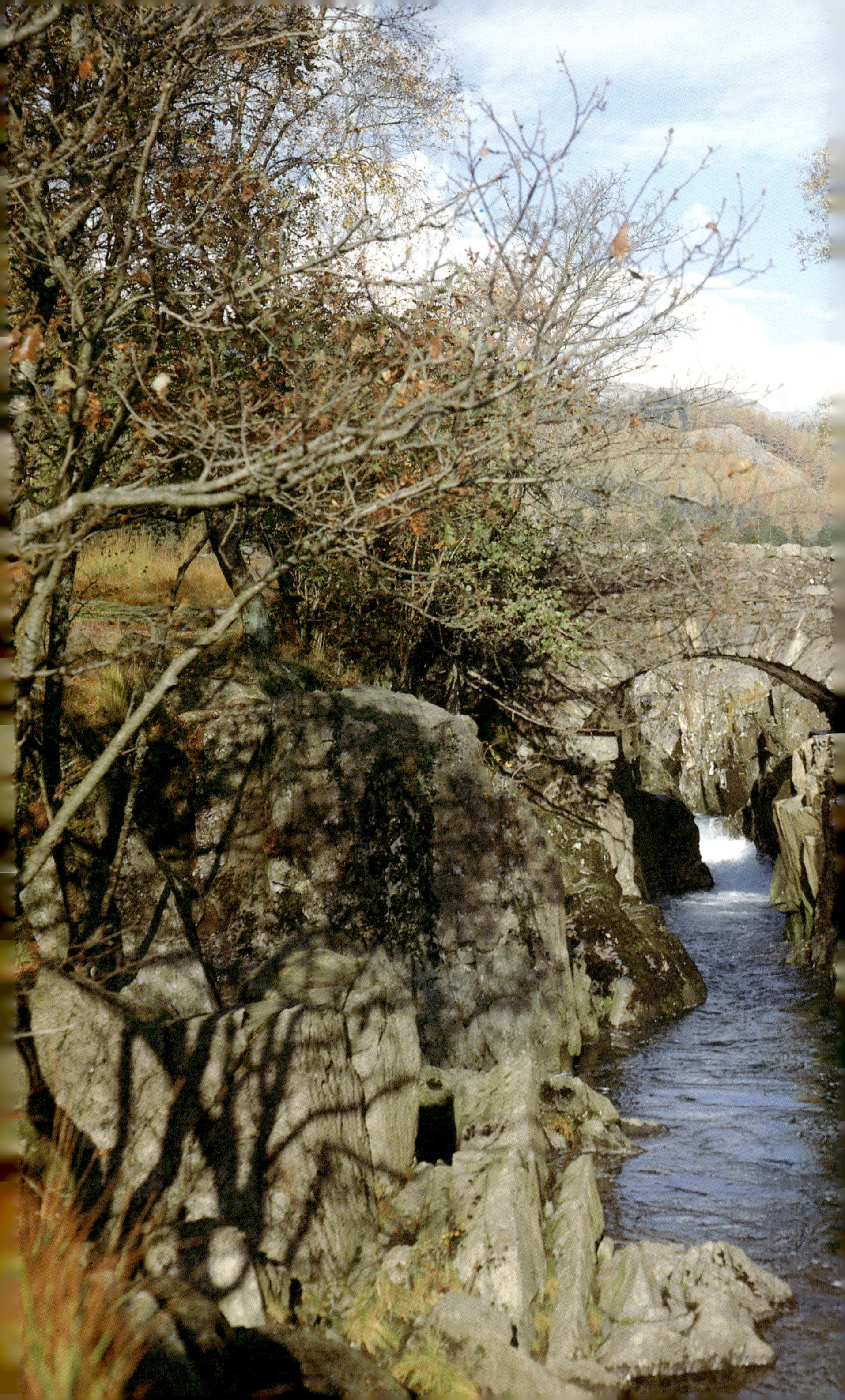

BIRKS BRIDGE spans the River Duddon by a favourite bathing spot. The word "birks" in Cumbrian place-names refers to birch trees, and these are still to be seen along the river bank, despite the Forestry Commission's fondness for the faster growing conifers which have been planted in the area.

The Kirk of Ulpha

The Kirk of Ulpha to the pilgrim's eye
Is welcome as a star, that doth present
Its shining forehead through the peaceful rent
Of a black cloud diffused o'er half the sky:
Or as a fruitful palm-tree towering high
O'er the parched waste beside an Arab's tent;
Or the Indian tree whose branches, downward bent,
Take root again, a boundless canopy.
How sweet were leisure! could it yield no more
Than 'mid that wave-washed Churchyard to recline,
From pastoral graves extracting thoughts divine;
Or there to pace, and mark the summits hoar
Of distant moon-lit mountains faintly shine,
Soothed by the unseen River's gentle roar.

After-Thought

I thought of Thee, my partner and my guide,
As being past away.–Vain sympathies!
For, backward, Duddon! as I cast my eyes,
I see what was, and is, and will abide;
Still glides the Stream, and shall for ever glide;
The Form remains, the Function never dies;
While we, the brave, the mighty, and the wise,
We Men, who in our morn of youth defied
The elements, must vanish;–be it so!
Enough, if something from your hands have power
To live, and act, and serve the future hour;
And if, as toward the silent tomb we go,
Through love, through hope, and faith's transcendent dower,
We feel that we are greater than we know.

    William Wordsworth *(from the River Duddon Sonnets)*

The Hayeswater Boat

A region desolate and wild,
Black, chafing water: and afloat,
And lonely as a truant child
In a waste wood, a single boat:
No mast, no sails are set thereon;
It moves, but never moveth on:

Behind, a buried vale doth sleep,
Far down the torrent cleaves its way:
In front the dumb rock rises steep,
A fretted wall of blue and grey;
All else, black water: and afloat,
One rood from shore, that single boat.

This boat they found against the shore:
The glossy rushes nodded by.
One rood from land they pushed, no more;
Then rested, listening silently.

Last night?–I looked, the sky was clear.
The boat was old, a battered boat.
In sooth, it seems a hundred year
Since that strange crew did ride afloat.
The boat hath drifted in the bay–
The oars have mouldered as they lay–
The rudder swings–yet none doth steer.
    What living hand hath brought it here?

    Matthew Arnold

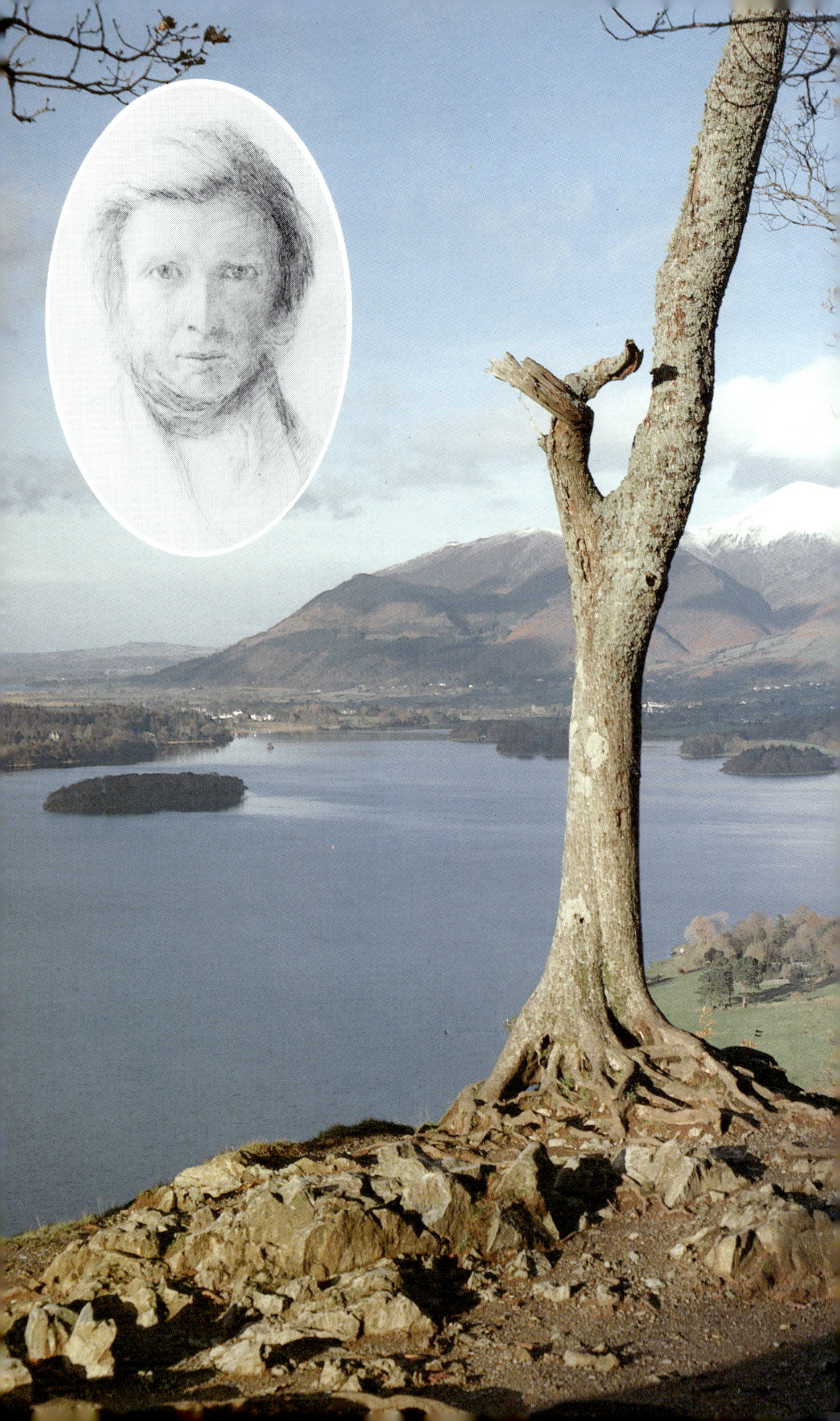

Yearning for the Lakes

I weary for the fountain foaming,
For shady holm and hill,
My mind is on the mountain roaming
My spirit's voice is still.

I weary for the woodland brook
That wanders through the vale,
I weary for the heights that look
Adown upon the dale.

The crags are lone on Coniston
And Glaramara's dell,
And dreary on the mighty one
The cloud enwreathed Sca-fell.

Oh, what although the crags are stern,
Their mighty peaks that sever,
Fresh flies the breeze on mountain fern
And free on mountain heather.

I long to tread the mountain head
Above the valley swelling,
I long to feel the breezes sped
From grey and gaunt Helvellyn.

There is a thrill of strange delight
That passes quivering o'er me,
When blue hills rise upon the sight
Like summer clouds before me.

  John Ruskin

SURPRISE VIEW is justly famous and aptly named, giving dizzying vistas across Derwentwater for travellers taking the exciting road from Borrowdale up to Watendlath Tarn.

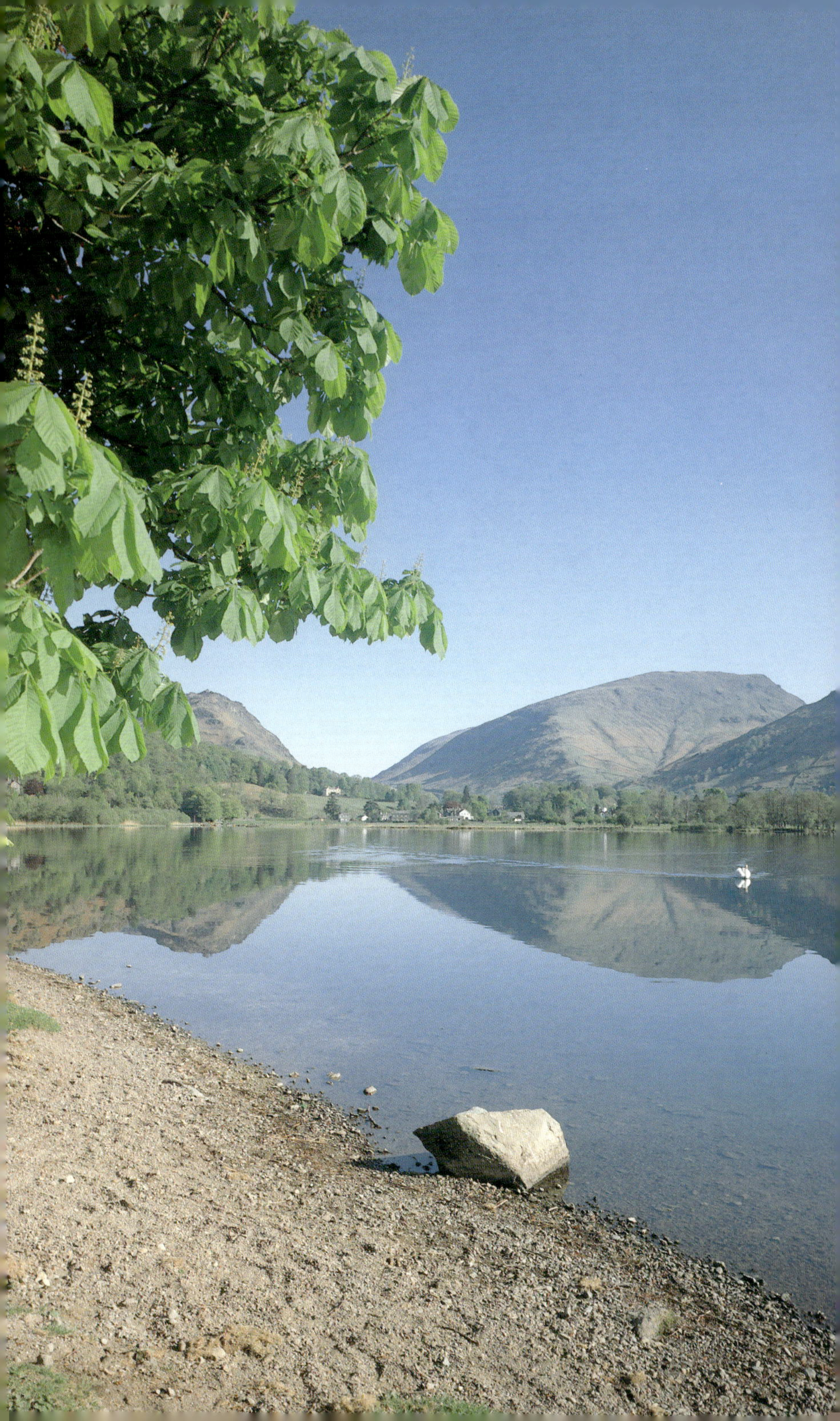

A Memory of Grasmere

O vale and lake, within your mountain-urn
Smiling tranquilly, and set so deep!
Oft doth your dreamy loveliness return,
Colouring the tender shadows of my sleep
With light Elysian; for the hues that steep
Your shores in melting lustre, seem to float
On golden clouds from spirit-lands remote,
Isles of the blest; and in our memory keep
Their place with holiest harmonies, Fair scene,
Most loved by evening and her dewy star!
Oh! ne'er may man, with touch unhallowed jar
The perfect music of thy charm serene!
Still, still unchanged, may *one* sweet region wear
Smiles that subdue the soul to love, and tears, and prayer.

    Felicia Dorothea Hemans

GRASMERE LAKE AND ISLAND: Wordsworth and his family and friends often enjoyed a rowing boat excursion to the island in the middle of Grasmere where they would brew tea and eat freshly caught pike. Today rowing boats can be hired from the tea gardens at Pavement End and a row out to the island is a guaranteed way of achieving peace and solitude even on the busiest day of summer. Less energetic visitors are content to remain on shore by the boat landings, drinking tea and drinking in the lovely views. On the outskirts of the village at Town End is Dove Cottage, Wordsworth's home from 1799 to 1808.

Beside the Mountain Rill

Shall I sing of little rills,
That trickle down the yellow hills,
To drive the Fairies' water-mills?–
Rills, upon whose pebbly brink,
Mountain birds may hop and drink–
Perching with a neck awry–
Darting upwards to the sky
The artless cunning of their eye–
Then away, away, away–
Up to the clouds that look so grey,
Away, Away, in the clear blue heaven,
Far o'er the thin mist that beneath is driven–
Now they sink, and now they soar,
Now poised upon the plumy oar,
Do they seek–at brightest noon,
For the light-inveiled moon?
Climbing upwards would they know
Where the stars at morning go?
If I err not–no–no–no–
Soar they high, or skim they low,
Every little bird has still
His heart beside the mountain rill.

    Hartley Coleridge

Mountain Tarns

O askest thou of me
What store of thoughtful glee
By mountain tarns is lying,
That I to such grim nooks
From my dull-hearted books
Should evermore be flying?

Go thou, and spend an hour
In autum fog and shower
Amid the thundering rills,
Or hear the breezy sigh
Of summer quiet die
Among the noonday hills.

. . . So I of lowly birth,
A workman on the earth,
Would cast myself apart,
That I a little time
From dreariness sublime
Might win a royal heart.

There is a power to bless
In hill-side loneliness,
In tarns and dreary places,
A virtue in the brook,
A freshness in the look
Of mountain's joyless faces.

And I would have my heart
From littleness apart,
A love-anointed thing,
Be set above my kind,
In my unfettered mind
A veritable king.

And so when life is dull,
Or when my heart is full
Because coy loves have frowned,
I wander up the rills
To stones and tarns and hills,-
I go there to be crowned.

    F.W. Faber

The Wanderer Returns

Once more I see thee, Skiddaw! once again
    Behold thee in thy majesty serene,
Where like the bulwark of this favour'd plain
    Alone thou standest, monarch of the scene:
Thou glorious Mountain, on whose ample breast
The sunbeams love to play, the vapours love to rest!

Once more, O Derwent, to thy aweful shores
    I come, insatiate of the accustom'd sight;
And listening as the eternal torrent roars,
    Drink in with eye and ear a fresh delight:
For I have wander'd far by land and sea,
In all my wandering still remembering thee.

And now am I a Cumbrian mountaineer;
    Their wintry garment of unsullied snow
The mountains have put on, the heavens are clear,
    And yon dark lake spreads silently below;
Who sees them only in their summer hour
Sees but their beauties half, and knows not half their power.

    Robert Southey

The Tables Turned

Up! up! my Friend, and quit your books;
Or surely you'll grow double:
Up! up! my Friend, and clear your looks;
Why all this toil and trouble?

The sun, above the mountain's head,
A freshening lustre mellow
Through all the long green fields has spread,
His first sweet evening yellow.

Books! 'tis a dull and endless strife:
Come, hear the woodland linnet,
How sweet his music! on my life,
There's more of wisdom in it.

And hark! how blithe the throstle sings!
He, too, is no mean preacher:
Come forth into the light of things,
Let Nature be your Teacher.

She has a world of ready wealth,
Our minds and hearts to bless–
Spontaneous wisdom breathed by health,
Truth breathed by cheerfulness.

One impulse from a vernal wood
May teach you more of man,
Of moral evil and of good,
Than all the sages can.

Sweet is the lore which Nature brings;
Our meddling intellect
Mis-shapes the beauteous forms of things:–
We murder to dissect.

Enough of Science and of Art;
Close up those barren leaves;
Come forth, and bring with you a heart
That watches and receives

    William Wordsworth

Sunset over the Langdale Pikes

... there the sun himself,
At the calm close of summer's longest day,
Rests his substantial orb;– between those heights
And on the top of either pinnacle,
More keenly than elsewhere in night's blue vault,
Sparkle the stars, as of their station proud.

William Wordsworth *(from* The Excursion Book II*)*

Blea Tarn House, Little Langdale

We scaled, without a track to ease our steps,
A steep ascent; and reached a dreary plain,
With a tumultuous waste of huge hill tops
Before us; savage region! which I paced
Dispirited: when, all at once, behold!
Beneath our feet, a little lowly vale,
A lowly vale, and yet uplifted high
Among the mountains; even as if the spot
Had been from eldest time by wish of theirs
So placed, to be shut out from all the world!
Urn-like it was in shape, deep as an urn;
With rocks encompassed, save that to the south
Was one small opening, where a heath-clad ridge
Supplied a boundary less abrupt and close;
A quiet treeless nook, with two green fields,
A liquid pool that glittered in the sun,
And one bare dwelling; one abode, no more!
It seemed the home of poverty and toil,
Though not of want: the little fields, made green
By husbandry of many thrifty years,
Paid cheerful tribute to the moorland house.
–There crows the cock, single in his domain:
The small birds find in spring no thicket there
To shroud them; only from the neighbouring vales
The cuckoo, straggling up to the hill tops,
Shouteth faint tidings of some gladder place.

Ah! what a sweet Recess, thought I, is here!
Instantly throwing down my limbs at ease
Upon a bed of heath;–full many a spot
Of hidden beauty have I chanced to espy
Among the mountains; never one like this;
So lonesome and so perfectly secure.

    William Wordsworth *(from 'The Excursion' Book II)*

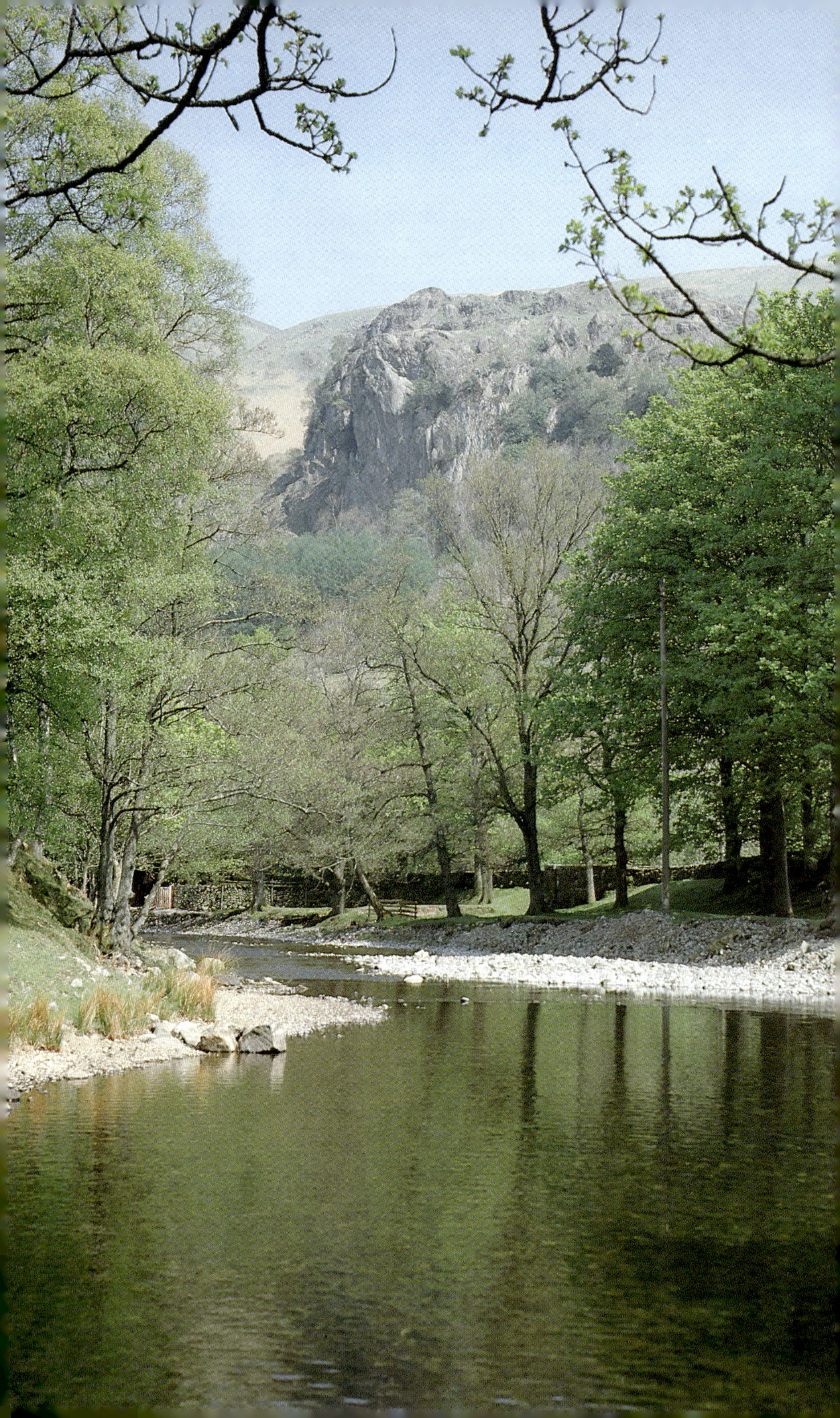

The Enchanted Castle of St John's Vale

Paled in by many a lofty hill,
The narrow dale lay smooth and still,
And, down its verdant bosom led,
A winding brooklet found its bed.
But, midmost of the vale, a mound
Arose with airy turrets crown'd,
Buttress, and rampire's circling bound,
    And mighty keep and tower;

Seem'd some primeval giant's hand
The castle's massive walls had plann'd,
A ponderous bulwark to withstand
    Ambitious Nimrod's power.
Above the moated entrance slung,
The balanced drawbridge trembling hung,
    As jealous of a foe;
Wicket of oak, as iron hard,
With iron studded, clench'd, and barr'd,
And prong'd portcullis, join'd to guard
    The gloomy pass below.
But the grey walls no banners crown'd,
Upon the watch-tower's airy round
No warder stood his horn to sound,
No guard beside the bridge was found,
And, where the Gothic gateway frown'd,
    Glanced neither bill nor bow.

Know, too, that when a pilgrim strays,
In morning mist or evening maze,
    Along the mountain lone,
That fairy fortress often mocks
His gaze upon the castled rocks
    Of the Valley of Saint John;
But never man since brave De Vaux
    The charmed portal won.
'Tis now a vain illusive show,
That melts whene'er the sunbeams glow
    Or the fresh breeze hath blown.

    Walter Scott *(from 'The Bridal of Triermain')*

De Vaux Discovers the Castle of St John

De Vaux had mark'd the sunbeams set,
At eve, upon the coronet
    Of that enchanted mound,
And seen but crags at random flung,
That, o'er the brawling torrent hung,
    In desolation frown'd.
What sees he by that meteor's lour?
A banner'd Castle, keep, and tower,
    Return the lurid gleam,
With battled walls and buttress fast,
And barbican and ballium vast,
And airy flanking towers, that cast
    Their shadows on the stream.

'Tis no deceit! distinctly clear
Crenell and parapet appear,
While o'er the pile that meteor drear
    Makes momentary pause;
Then forth its solemn path it drew,
And fainter yet and fainter grew
Those gloomy towers upon the view,
    As its wild light withdraws.

Forth from the cave did Roland rush,
O'er crag and stream, through brier and bush;
    Yet far he had not sped
Ere sunk was that portentous light
Behind the hills, and utter night
    Was on the valley spread.
He paused perforce, and blew his horn,
And on the mountain-echoes borne,
    Was heard an answering sound,
A wild and lonely trumpet-note;
In middle air it seem'd to float
    High o'er the battled mound;
And sounds were heard, as when a guard
Of some proud castle, holding ward,
    Pace forth their nightly round.
The valiant Knight of Triermain
Rung forth his challenge-blast again,

But answer came there none;
And 'mid the mingled wind and rain,
Darkling he sought the vale in vain,
　　Until the dawning shone;
And when it dawn'd, that wondrous sight,
Distinctly seen by meteor light–
　　It all had pass'd away;
And that enchanted mount once more
A pile of granite fragments bore,
　　As at the close of day.

Steel'd for the deed, De Vaux's heart
Scorn'd from his vent'rous quest to part,
　　He walks the vale once more;
But only sees, by night or day,
That shatter'd pile of rocks so grey,
　　Hears but the torrent's roar.
Till when, through hills of azure borne,
The moon renew'd her silver horn
Just at the time her waning ray
Had faded in the dawning day,
　　A summer mist arose;
Adown the vale the vapours float,
And cloudy undulations moat
That tufted mound of mystic note,
　　As round its base they close.
And higher now the fleecy tide
Ascends its stern and shaggy side,
Until the airy billows hide
　　The rock's majestic isle;
It seem'd a veil of filmy lawn,
By some fantastic fairy drawn
　　Around enchanted pile.
The breeze came softly down the brook,
　　And, sighing as it blew,
The veil of silver mist it shook,
And to De Vaux's eager look
　　Renew'd that wondrous view.
For, though the loitering vapour braved
The gentle breeze, yet oft it waved
　　Its mantle's dewy fold;

And still, when shook that filmy screen,
Were towers and bastions dimly seen,
And Gothic battlements between
    Their gloomy length unroll'd.
Speed, speed, De Vaux, ere on thine eye
Once more the fleeting vision die!
    The gallant knight 'gan speed
As prompt and light as, when the hound
Is opening, and the horn is wound,
    Careers the hunter's steed.
Down the steep dell his course amain
    Hath rivall'd archer's shaft;
But ere the mound he could attain,
The rocks their shapeless form regain,
And, mocking loud his labour vain,
    The mountain spirits laugh'd.
Far up the echoing dell was borne
Their wild unearthly shout of scorn.

Wroth wax'd the Warrior: 'Am I then
Fool'd by the enemies of men,
Like a poor hind, whose homeward way
Is haunted by malicious fay?
Is Triermain become your taunt,
De Vaux your scorn? False fiends, avaunt!'
A weighty curtal-axe he bare;
The baleful blade so bright and square,
And the tough shaft of heben wood,
Were oft in Scottish gore imbrued.
Backward his stately form he drew,
And at the rocks the weapon threw,
Just where one crag's projected crest
Hung proudly balanced o'er the rest.
Hurl'd with main force, the weapon's shock
Rent a huge fragment of the rock.
If by mere strength, 'twere hard to tell,
Or if the blow dissolved some spell,
But down the headlong ruin came,
With cloud of dust and flash of flame.
Down bank, o'er bush, its course was borne,
Crush'd lay the copse, the earth was torn,
Till staid at length, the ruin dread
Cumber'd the torrent's rocky bed,

And bade the waters' high swoln tide
Seek other passage for its pride.

When ceased that thunder, Triermain
Survey'd the mound's rude front again;
And, lo! the ruin had laid bare,
Hewn in the stone, a winding stair,
Whose moss'd and fractured steps might lend
The means the summit to ascend;
And by whose aid the brave De Vaux
Began to scale these magic rocks,
    And soon a platform won,
Where, the wild witchery to close,
Within three lances' length arose
    The Castle of Saint John!
No misty phantom of the air,
No meteor-blazon'd show was there;
In morning splendour, full and fair,
    The massive fortress shone.

    Walter Scott *(from 'The Bridal of Triermain')*

CASTLE ROCK, LEGBURTHWAITE: *just along the B5322 from the main A591 a large rock outcrop dominates the southern end of the Vale of St John. The eighteenth century historian William Hutchinson reported that the inhabitants living close to this rock believed it to be "an antediluvian structure" and legend asserts that the rock is in fact an enchanted fortress, best viewed from the north, with rock formations taking on the appearance of "lofty turrets and ragged battlements". Scott's description in "The Bridal of Triermain" seems to have compounded its fame, so that some modern maps actually name it "Castle Rock of Triermain". A picnic site and car park close to the road junction is a good vantage point from which to observe climbers attempting the rock buttress. (See page 40).*

SKIDDAW AND DERWENTWATER: Skiddaw is the fourth highest hill in Lakeland seen here from the famous Ashness Bridge viewpoint. An average walker can be up and down Skiddaw in three hours, and keen fell runners can achieve the return trip from Keswick in just over one hour. On a clear day it is the most straightforward of the high peaks to ascend, and its prominent summit provides extensive views. It was this prominence which made it such a suitable location for the warning beacons which were lit in troubled times. Beacons are still constructed on occasions of national celebration, such as the Queen's Silver Jubilee in 1977.

Descent of Skiddaw

On the verge of the hill we precariously stood
And, awe-struck, we gazed on the far-rolling flood.
Eternally murmuring, distant, and deep,
It stretched its cœrulean waves at our feet.
Delighted and eagerly catching the view,
Our swift, eager eyes round the prospect we threw;
And, although in a cutting and cold situation,
We cared not to move from our high elevation,–
So, blowing our fingers and blowing our nose,
Not minding the cold that was pinching our toes,
And combating weather, and combating wind,
Still, still, at the summit, we lingered behind.
But as all of us knew, 'twas in vain to lament,–
So cheerfully all, we began the descent.
But as it was difficult, stoney, and steep
We judged it was better to trust to our feet,
And as none of us chose down the mountain to ride,
We left all our steeds to the care of the guide.
Now upon the descent I can not say much more
Unless I describe what I've told of before.
We came to the halting place,–past by the rill,–
And mounted our steeds at the foot of the hill.
We forced through the bog, and we came to the dell
Where the murmurs of that sparkling rivulet swell,–
Rode round about Latrigg,–to th' river came down,
And at last we did safely arrive in the town.
Now tell me, O reader, hast tasted repose
When toilings and labours have come to a close?
Hast thou gloried when thou hast successfully toiled
In overgrown dangers and diff'culties foiled?
Oh, then and then only, thou fitly canst tell
How our hearts lightly beat and our proud bosoms swell.
Delighted we sat round the bright blazing fire,
And talked of our hardships,–the mountain, the mire.
Though other things sink in the chaos of thought,
And fly from our mem'ry, let all be forgot,
As light chaff is borne on the face of the wind,
Yet Skiddaw shall ne'er be erased from our mind.

    John Ruskin *(aged eleven) from 'Iteriad'.*

A Fell Walk

We left, just ten years since, you say,
That wayside inn we left to-day.
Our jovial host, as forth we fare,
Shouts greeting from his easy chair.
High on a bank our leader stands,
Reviews and ranks his motley bands,
Makes clear our goal to every eye–
The valley's western boundary.
A gate swings to! our tide hath flowed
Already from the silent road.
The valley-pastures, one by one,
Are threaded, quiet in the sun;
And now beyond the rude stone bridge
Slopes gracious up the western ridge.
Its woody border, and the last
Of its dark upland farms is past–
Cool farms, with open-lying stores,
Under their burnished sycamores;
All past! and through the trees we glide,
Emerging on the green hill-side.
There climbing hangs, a far-seen sign,
Our wavering, many-coloured line;
There winds, upstreaming slowly still
Over the summit of the hill.
And now, in front, behold outspread
Those upper regions we must tread!
Mild hollows, and clear heathy swells,
The cheerful silence of the fells.
Some two hours' march with serious air,
Through the deep noontide heats we fare;
The red-grouse, springing at our sound,
Skims, now and then, the shining ground;
No life, save his and ours, intrudes
Upon these breathless solitudes.

    Matthew Arnold *(from 'Resignation')*

Wytheburn Chapel and Inn

Here, traveller, pause and think, and duly think
    What happy, holy thoughts may heavenward rise
Whilst thou and thy good steed together drink
    Beneath this little portion of the skies.

See! on one side, a humble house of prayer,
    Where silence dwells, a maid immaculate,
Save when the Sabbath and the priest are there,
    And some few hungry souls for manna wait.

Humble it is and meek and very low,
    And speaks its purpose by a single bell;
And God Himself, and He alone, can know
If spiry temples please him half so well.

Then see the World, the world in its best guise,
    Inviting thee its bounties to partake;
Dear is the Sign's old time-discoloured dyes
    To weary trudger by the long black lake.

And pity 'tis that other studded door
    That looks so rusty right across the way,
Stands not always as was the use of yore,
    That whoso passes may step in and pray.

    Hartley Coleridge

CASTLERIGG STONE CIRCLE is a magnificently positioned collection of forty-eight stones erected approximately 3,500 years ago. Nineteenth Century artists and writers erroneously described it as a Druid's Circle. Its precise purpose and origins are unknown, but its dramatic setting is beyond dispute. When the young Wordsworth and Coleridge visited it on their walking tour of 1799 they found that vandals from Keswick had whitewashed the stones. When the field containing the circle came on to the market in 1913 Canon Rawnsley (whose poems are represented in this anthology) organised the fund-raising campaign to purchase the property for the National Trust.

> . . . like a dismal cirque
> Of Druid stones, upon a forlorn moor,
> When the chill rain begins at shut of eve,
> In dull November, and their chancel vault,
> The Heaven itself, is blinded throughout night.
>
> John Keats *(from 'Hyperion', Book 2)*

Thirlmere to Castlerigg

The dark, narrow Thirlmere lay low at our feet;
The huge hills reposed on the face of the deep.
Far, far 'neath its waters inverted they stood,
And rolled o'er their imaged summits the flood.
We could scarcely imagine the lake there to flow,
And waters to roll and to murmur below
So smooth and so glassy the lake, that beneath
A deep rocky valley we seemed to perceive.
How bright,–how luxuriant, looked the thick heath,
Its rich purple bells as 'twas bending beneath,
Its patches rich shaded with fern as it grew,
And mantled the hill with is Tyrian hue.
While, beyond, a dark chaos of mountains was tost,
And hills after hills in the distance were lost:
While the sun, ere he died on the mountains away,
Was shedding its brightest,–but transient–ray.
Now reaching our carriage, with lingering look,
Of Helvellyn and Thirlmere our farewell we took;
By rock and by brooklet swift galloping on,
And holding our course by the Vale of St John,
As the sun was just setting, and late was the time,
We hastened tall Castlerig's windings to climb.
As some people say, I believe it is true–
Though its presence I can't say that I ever knew–
A druidical temple is built on its top,
A circle of nature-hewn masses of rock.
Upon admiration these may have some claims,
As the buildings of old and ancestral remains
When each savage lived free and fierce and unknown,
The wild his dominion, the forest his home.
I revere and I honour a temple, as such,
And gazing in wonder admire it full much,–
But I care not at all for a great set of stones
Which are bidding you always beware of your bones
For fear of a tumble! Although very fine things,
I think some great giant was playing at ninepins,–
And leaving the place, ere his ball he could swing,
Has left all his ninepins stuck up in a ring!

    John Ruskin (aged eleven) *(from 'Iteriad')*

The Knight's Tomb

Where is the grave of Sir Arthur O'Kellyn?
Where may the grave of that good man be?–
By the side of a spring, on the breast of Helvellyn,
Under the twigs of a young birch tree!
The oak that in summer was sweet to hear,
And rustled its leaves in the fall of the year,
And whistled and roared in the winter alone,
Is gone,–and the birch in its stead is grown.–
The knight's bones are dust,
And his good sword rust;–
His soul is with the saints, I trust.

Stern Blencartha

On stern Blencartha's perilous height
    The winds are tyrannous and strong;
And flashing forth unsteady light
From stern Blencartha's skiey height,
    As loud the torrents throng!
Beneath the moon, in gentle weather
They blend the earth and sky together.
But oh! the sky and all its forms how quiet!
The things that seek the earth, how full of noise and riot!

    Samuel Taylor Coleridge

Savage Grandeur

Horrors like these at first alarm,
But soon with savage grandeur charm,
And raise to noblest thoughts the mind:
Thus by thy fall, Lowdore reclin'd,
The craggy cliff, impending wood,
Whose shadows mix o'er half the flood,
The gloomy clouds, which solemn sail,
Scarce lifted by the languid gale,
O'er the capp'd hill, the dark'ned vale;
The rav'ning kite, and bird of Jove,
Which round the aerial ocean rove,
And, floating on the billowy sky,
With full expanded pinions fly,
Their flutt'ring or their bleating prey
Thence with death-dooming eye survey;
Channels by rocky torrents torn,
Rocks to the lake in thunders borne,
Or such as o'er our heads appear
Suspended in their mid-career,
To start again at his command
Who rules fire, water, air and land,
I view with wonder and delight.

    John Dalton *(from 'Sweet Keswick Vale')*.

The Cataract of Lodore

"How does the Water
Come down at Lodore?"
My little boy ask'd me
Thus, once on a time;
And moreover he task'd me
To tell him in rhyme.
Anon at the word,
There first came one daughter
And then came another,
To second and third
The request of their brother,
And to hear how the water
Comes down to Lodore,
With its rush and its roar.
As many a time
They had seen it before.
So I told them in rhyme,
For of rhymes I had store:
And 'twas in my vocation
For their recreation
That so I should sing;
Because I was Laureate
To them and the King.

From its sources which well
In the Tarn on the fell;
From its fountains
In the mountains,
Its rills and its gills;
Through moss and through brake,
It runs and it creeps
For awhile, till it sleeps
In its own little Lake.
And thence at departing,
Awakening and starting,
It runs through the reeds
And away it proceeds,
Through meadow and glade,
In sun and in shade,
And through the wood-shelter,
Among crags in its flurry,

Helter-skelter,
Hurry-scurry.
Here it comes sparkling,
And there it lies darkling;
Now smoaking and frothing
It's tumult and wrath in,
Till in this rapid race
On which it is bent,
It reaches the place
Of its steep descent.

The cataract strong
Then plunges along,
Striking and raging
As if a war waging
Its caverns and rocks among:
Rising and leaping,
Sinking and creeping,
Swelling and sweeping
Showering and springing,
Flying and flinging,
Writhing and ringing,
Eddying and whisking,
Spouting and frisking,
Turning and twisting,
Around and around
With endless rebound!
Smiting and fighting,
A sight to delight in;
Confounding, astounding,
Dizzying and deafening the ear with its sound.

Collecting, projecting,
Receding and speeding,
And shocking and rocking,
And darting and parting,
And threading and spreading,
And whizzing and hissing,
And dripping and skipping,
And hitting and splitting,
And shining and twining,
And rattling and battling,
And shaking and quaking,
And pouring and roaring,

And waving and raving,
And tossing and crossing,
And flowing and going,
And running and stunning,
And foaming and roaming,
And dinning and spinning,
And dropping and hopping,
And working and jerking,
And guggling and struggling,
And heaving and cleaving,
And moaning and groaning;

And glittering and frittering,
And gathering and feathering,
And whitening and brightening,
And quivering and shivering,
And hurrying and scurrying,
And thundering and floundering;

Dividing and gliding and sliding,
And falling and brawling and sprawling,
And driving and riving and striving,
And sprinkling and twinkling and wrinkling,
And sounding and bounding and rounding,
And bubbling and troubling and doubling,
And grumbling and rumbling and tumbling,
And clattering and battering and shattering;

Retreating and beating and meeting and sheeting,
Delaying and straying and playing and spraying,
Advancing and prancing and glancing and dancing,
Recoiling, turmoiling and toiling and boiling,
And gleaming and streaming and steaming and beaming,
And rushing and flushing and brushing and gushing,
And flapping and rapping and clapping and slapping,
And curling and whirling and purling and twirling,
And thumping and plumping and bumping and jumping,
And dashing and flashing and splashing and clashing,
And so never ending, but always descending,
Sounds and motions for ever and ever are blending,
All at once and all o'er, with a mighty uproar,
And this way the Water comes down at Lodore.

    Robert Southey

Hellvellyn

I climb'd the dark brow of the mighty Hellvellyn,
    Lakes and mountains beneath me gleam'd misty and wide;
All was still, save by fits, when the eagle was yelling,
    And starting around me the echoes replied.
On the right, Striden-edge round the Red-tarn was bending,
And Catchedicam its left verge was defending,
One huge nameless rock in the front was ascending,
    When I mark'd the sad spot where the wanderer had died.

Dark green was that spot 'mid the brown mountain-heather,
    Where the Pilgrim of Nature lay stretch'd in decay,
Like the corpse of an outcast abandon'd to weather,
    Till the mountain winds wasted the tenantless clay.
Nor yet quite deserted, though lonely extended,
For, faithful in death, his mute favourite attended,
The much-loved remains of her master defended,
    And chased the hill-fox and the raven away.

How long didst thou think that this silence was slumber?
    When the wind waved his garment, how oft didst thou start?
How many long days and long weeks didst thou number,
    Ere he faded before thee, the friend of thy heart?
And, oh, was it meet, that–no requiem read o'er him–
No mother to weep, and no friend to deplore him,
And thou, little guardian, alone stretch'd before him–
    Unhonour'd the Pilgrim from life should depart?

When a Prince to the fate of the Peasant has yielded,
    The tapestry waves dark round the dim-lighted hall;
With scutcheons of silver the coffin is shielded,
    And pages stand mute by the canopied pall:
Through the courts, at deep midnight, the torches are gleaming;
In the proudly-arch'd chapel the banners are beaming,
Far adown the long aisle sacred music is streaming,
    Lamenting a Chief of the people should fall.

But meeter for thee, gentle lover of nature,
    To lay down thy head like the meek mountain lamb,
When, wilder'd, he drops from some cliff huge in stature,
    And draws his last sob by the side of his dam.

And more stately thy couch by this desert lake lying,
Thy obsequies sung by the grey plover flying,
With one faithful friend but to witness thy dying,
    In the arms of Hellvellyn and Catchedicam.

    Walter Scott.

HELVELLYN: the third highest hill in England and the most popular of Lakeland's high fells with walkers. But it is a walk not to be underestimated, as the annual statistics of fell accidents repeatedly demonstrate. Both Wordsworth's poem "Fidelity" and Scott's "Hellvellyn" refer to a particularly notable fatality which occurred in April 1805 when Charles Gough, a young gentleman-artist, fell to his death near Red Tarn. Gough's terrier bitch guarded her master's corpse until it was discovered a full three months later. By then the terrier had become semi wild and given birth to a litter of puppies. Scott and Wordsworth climbed Helvellyn that same year in the company of Humphry Davy, the distinguished scientist. Apparently both poets worked on their poems quite independently and unknown to each other.

Fidelity

A barking sound the Shepherd hears,
A cry as of a dog or fox;
He halts–and searches with his eyes
Among the scattered rocks:
And now at distance can discern
A stirring in a brake of fern;
And instantly a dog is seen,
Glancing through that covert green.

The Dog is not of mountain breed;
Its motions, too, are wild and shy;
With something, as the Shepherd thinks,
Unusual in its cry:
Nor is there any one in sight
All round, in hollow or on height;
Nor shout, nor whistle strikes his ear;
What is the creature doing here?

It was a cove, a huge recess,
That keeps, till June, December's snow;
A lofty precipice in front,
A silent tarn below!
Far in the bosom of Helvellyn,
Remote from public road or dwelling,
Pathway, or cultivated land;
From trace of human foot or hand.

There sometimes doth a leaping fish
Send through the tarn a lonely cheer;
The crags repeat the raven's croak,
In symphony austere:
Thither the rainbow comes–the cloud–
And mists that spread the flying shroud:
And sunbeams; and the sounding blast,
That, if it could, would hurry past;
But that enormous barrier holds it fast.

Not free from boding thoughts, a while
The Shepherd stood; then makes his way
O'er rocks and stones, following the Dog
As quickly as he may;
Nor far had gone before he found
A human skeleton on the ground;
The appalled Discoverer with a sigh
Looks round, to learn the history.

From those abrupt and perilous rocks
The Man had fallen, that place of fear!
At length upon the Shepherd's mind
It breaks, and all is clear:
He instantly recalled the name,
And who he was, and whence he came;
Remembered, too, the very day
On which the Traveller passed this way.

But hear a wonder, for whose sake
This lamentable tale I tell!
A lasting monument of words
This wonder merits well.
The Dog, which still was hovering nigh,
Repeating the same timid cry,
This Dog, had been through three months space
A dweller in that savage place.

Yes, proof was plain that, since the day
When this ill-fated Traveller died,
The Dog had watched about the spot,
Or by his master's side:
How nourished here through such long time
He knows, who gave that love sublime;
And gave that strength of feeling, great
Above all human estimate!

    William Wordsworth.

KIRKSTONE PASS *takes its name from the church-like boulder near the summit, providing a striking landmark when seen silhouetted against the sky. De Quincey estimated that a carriage from this point could descend into Patterdale at a rate of eighteen miles an hour: "a real luxury for those who enjoy the velocity of motion". The ascent from Ambleside to Kirkstone is known as "the Struggle" and the Pass easily becomes blocked by snow — to the delight of skiers who can often be seen in winter.*

The Pass of Kirkstone

Within the mind strong fancies work,
A deep delight the bosom thrills,
Oft as I pass along the fork
Of these fraternal hills:

Where, save the rugged road, we find
No appanage of human kind,
Nor hint of man; if stone or rock
Seem not his handy-work to mock
By something cognizably shaped;
Mockery–or model roughly hewn,
And left as if by earthquake strewn,
Or from the Flood escaped:
Altars for Druid service fit;
Wrinkled Egyptian monument;
Green moss-grown tower; or hoary tent;
Tents of a camp that never shall be razed–
On which four thousand years have gazed!

Ye ploughshares sparkling on the slopes!
Ye snow-white lambs that trip
Imprisoned 'mid the formal props
Of restless ownership!
Ye trees, that may to-morrow fall
To feed the insatiate Prodigal!
Lawns, houses, chattels, groves, and fields,
All that the fertile valley shields;
Wages of folly–baits of crime,
Of life's uneasy game the stake,
Playthings that keep the eyes awake
Of drowsy, dotard Time;–
O care! O guilt!–O vales and plains,
Here, 'mid his own unvexed domains,
A Genius dwells, that can subdue
At once all memory of You,–
Most potent when mists veil the sky,
Mists that distort and magnify,
While the coarse rushes, to the sweeping breeze,
Sigh forth their ancient melodies!

    William Wordsworth.

To a Rainbow

My heart leaps up when I behold
    A rainbow in the sky:
So was it when my life began;
So is it now I am a man;
So be it when I shall grow old,
    Or let me die!
The Child is father of the Man;
And I could wish my days to be
Bound each to each by natural piety.

    William Wordsworth

Airey-Force Valley

Not a breath of air
Ruffles the bosom of this leafy glen.
From the brook's margin, wide around, the trees
Are steadfast as the rocks; the brook itself,
Old as the hills that feed it from afar,
Doth rather deepen than disturb the calm
Where all things else are still and motionless.
And yet, even now, a little breeze, perchance
Escaped from boisterous winds that rage without,
Has entered, by the sturdy oaks unfelt,
But to its gentle touch how sensitive
Is the light ash! that, pendent from the brow
Of yon dim cave, in seeming silence makes
A soft eye-music of slow-waving boughs,
Powerful almost as vocal harmony
To stay the wanderer's steps and soothe his thoughts.

    William Wordsworth.

Midnight Adoration

"Beneath the full-orb'd moon, that bathed in light
    The mellow'd verdure of Helvellyn's steep,
My spirit teeming with creations bright,
    I walked like one who wanders in his sleep!

"The glittering stillness of the starry sky
    Shone in my heart as in the waveless sea;
And rising up in kindred majesty
    I felt my soul from earthly fetters free!

"Joy filled my being like a gentle flood;
    I felt as living without pulse or breath,
Eternity seem'd o'er my heart to brood,
    And as a faded dream, I thought of death.

"Through the hush'd air awoke mysterious awe,
    God cheer'd my loneliness with holy mirth,
And in this blended mood I clearly saw
    The moving spirit that pervades the earth.

"While adoration blessed my inward sense
    I felt how beautiful this world could be,
When clothed with gleams of high intelligence
    Born of the mountain's still sublimity.

"I sunk in silent worship on my knees,
    While night's unnumber'd planets roll'd afar;
Blest moment for a contrite heart to seize–
    Forgiving love shone forth in every star!

"The mighty moon my pensive soul subdued
    With sorrow, tranquil as her cloudless ray,
Mellowing the transport of her loftiest mood
    With conscious glimmerings of immortal day.

"I felt with pain that life's perturbed wave
    Had dimm'd the blaze to sinless spirits given
But saw with joy, reposing on the grave,
    The seraph Hope that points the way to heaven.

"The waveless clouds that hung amid the light,
    By Mercy's hand with braided glory wove,
Seem'd in their boundless mansions, to my sight
    Like guardian spirits o'er the land they love.

"My heart lay pillowed on their wings of snow,
    Drinking the calm that slept on every fold,
Till memory of the life she led below
    Seem'd like a tragic tale to pity told.

"When visions from the distant world arose–
    How fair the gleams from memory's mystic urn!
How did my soul, 'mid Nature's blest repose,
    To the soft bosom of affection turn!

"Then sinless grew my hopes, my wishes pure,
    Breeding a seraph loftiness of soul;
Though free from pride, I felt of heaven secure,
    A step, a moment from the eternal goal:

"Those fearful doubts that strike the living blood,
    Those dreams that sink the heart, we know not why,
Were changed to joy this mysterious mood,
    Sprung from the presence of Eternity.

"I saw, returning to its fount sublime,
    The flood of being that from Nature flowed;
And then, displaying at the death of time,
    The essence and the lineaments of God!

"Thus pass'd the midnight hour, till from the wave
    The orient sun flamed slowly up the sky;
Such a blest spirit found illumined gaze,
    And seem'd to realize my vision high."

    Christopher North.

Foxgloves at Brandelhow

Now lingers long the gold within the west,
   Now twilit daises shimmer silver-clear
   Pale as the moon upon the dewy mere
Where lilies sleep; the fern-clad mountain breast
Green to the sky, by white flocks is possess't,
   And elders bloom, and roses far and near
   Dance in the hedgerows, whilst, at dawn, I hear
The thrush sing loud about her second nest.

But neither daisied fields nor milk-white sheep,
   Nor rose, nor song of bird, nor elder flower,
     Nor hint of heather on the mountain's brow
   Can wield o'er wondering hearts such magic power
     As those tall foxglove spires, whose sceptres keep
Imperial sway for June in Brandelhow.

H D Rawnsley

From "The Prelude"

The gentle Banks
Of Emont, hitherto unnam'd in Song,
And that monastic Castle, on a Flat
Low-standing by the margin of the Stream,
A Mansion not unvisited of old
By Sidney, where, in sight of our Helvellyn,
Some snatches he might pen, for aught we know,
Of his Arcadia, by fraternal love
Inspir'd; that River and that mouldering Dome
Have seen us sit in many a summer hour,
My sister and myself, when having climb'd
In danger through some window's open space,
We look'd abroad, or on the Turret's head
Lay listening to the wild flowers and the grass,
As they gave out their whispers to the wind.
Another Maid there was, who also breath'd
A gladdness o'er that season, then to me
By her exulting outside look of youth
And placid under-countenance, first endear'd,
That other Spirit, Coleridge, who is now
So near to us, that meek confiding heart,
So reverenced by us both. O'er paths and fields
In all that neighbourhood, through narrow lanes
Of eglantine, and through the shady woods,
And o'er the Border Beacon, and the Waste
Of naked Pools, and common Crags that lay
Expos'd on the bare Fell, was scatter'd love,
A spirit of pleasure and youth's golden gleam.

William Wordsworth

BROUGHAM CASTLE: *one of Cumbria's finest historical monuments. The keep dates from the reign of Henry II and there is the site of a Roman fort close by. Visitors with a head for heights may scale the southwest tower and enjoy a truly exhilarating view. Wordsworth and his sister Dorothy played here as children. Lady Anne Clifford was the last notable occupant and a slab in the outer gatehouse records her importance: "Countess Dowager of Pembrook, Dorsett and Montgomery, Baroness Clifford, Westmorland and Vesete, Ladie of the Honour of Skipton in Craven, and High Sheriffesse, by inheritance, of the countie of Westmorland".*

To a Butterfly

I've watched you now a full half-hour,
Self-poised upon that yellow flower;
And, little Butterfly! indeed
I know not if you sleep or feed.
How motionless!–not frozen seas
More motionless! and then
What joy awaits you, when the breeze
Hath found you out among the trees,
And calls you forth again!

This plot of orchard-ground is ours;
My trees they are, my Sister's flowers;
Here rest your wings when they are weary;
Here lodge as in a sanctuary!
Come often to us, fear no wrong;
Sit near us on the bough!
We'll talk of sunshine and of song,
And summer days, when we were young;
Sweet childish days, that were as long
As twenty days are now.

William Wordsworth.

Heather on Lonscale

AUG. 18th

God, for the gift of the thunder and fire I fear Thee,
    –Gift of the thunder and fire that gave us our fells;
But for the gift of this wonder my love comes anear Thee,
    Gift of the wonder of these multitudinous bells.
Oh! the sweet scent and the dust of the honey around me–
    Oh! the sweet sound of the brindled and golden thighed bees,
Oh! the content which on Lonscale's round shoulder has found me.
    Rest that has found me where body and soul are at ease.

H.D. Rawnsley

Yew Trees

There is a Yew-tree, pride of Lorton Vale,
Which to this day stands single, in the midst
Of its own darkness, as it stood of yore:
Not loth to furnish weapons for the bands
Of Umfraville or Percy ere they marched
To Scotland's heaths; or those that crossed the sea
And drew their sounding bows at Azincour,
Perhaps at earlier Crecy, or Poictiers.
Of vast circumference and gloom profound
This solitary Tree! a living thing
Produced too slowly ever to decay;
Of form and aspect too magnificent
To be destroyed. But worthier still of note
Are those fraternal Four of Borrowdale,
Joined in one solemn and capacious grove;
Huge trunks! and each particular trunk a growth
Of intertwisted fibres serpentine
Up-coiling, and inveterately convolved;
Nor uninformed with Phantasy, and looks
That threaten the profane; a pillared shade,
Upon whose grassless floor of red-brown hue,
By sheddings from the pining umbrage tinged
Perennially–beneath whose sable roof
Of boughs, as if for festal purpose decked
With unrejoicing berries–ghostly Shapes
May meet at noontide; Fear and trembling Hope,
Silence and Foresight; Death the Skeleton
And Time the Shadow;–there to celebrate,
As in a natural temple scattered o'er
With altars undisturbed of mossy stone,
United worship; or in mute repose
To lie, and listen to the mountain flood
Murmuring from Glaramara's inmost caves.

    William Wordsworth

Skating on Esthwaite Water

And in the frosty season, when the sun
Was set, and visible for many a mile
The cottage windows blazed through twilight gloom,
I heeded not their summons: happy time
It was indeed for all of us–for me
It was a time of rapture! Clear and loud
The village clock tolled six,–I wheeled about,
Proud and exulting like an untired horse
That cares not for his home. All shod with steel,
We hissed along the polished ice in games
Confederate, imitative of the chase
And woodland pleasures,–the resounding horn,
The pack loud chiming, and the hunted hare.
So through the darkness and the cold we flew,
And not a voice was idle; with the din
Smitten, the precipices rang aloud;
The leafless trees and every icy crag
Tinkled like iron; while far distant hills
Into the tumult sent an alien sound
Of melancholy not unnoticed, while the stars
Eastward were sparkling clear, and in the west
The orange sky of evening died away.
Not seldom from the uproar I retired
Into a silent bay, or sportively
Glanced sideway, leaving the tumultuous throng,
To cut across the reflex of a star
That fled, and, flying still before me, gleamed
Upon the glassy plain; and oftentimes,
When we had given our bodies to the wind,
And all the shadowy banks on either side
Came sweeping through the darkness spinning still
The rapid line of motion, then at once
Have I, reclining back upon my heels,
Stopped short; yet still the solitary cliffs
Wheeled by me–even as if the earth had rolled
With visible motion her diurnal round!
Behind me did they stretch in solemn train,
Feebler and feebler, and I stood and watched
Till all was tranquil as a dreamless sleep.

William Wordsworth *(from 'The Prelude')*

HAWKSHEAD CHURCH *occupies a fine elevated site surrounded by picturesque old buildings. Among the curiosities on display inside is a burial in woollen certificate from the days when Parliament sought to encourage the wool trade. witnesses testify that "the corps was nott put in or wound up or buried in any shirt, shift, sheet or shroud made or mingled with flax hempe silke haire gold or silver or other than what is made of sheep's wool onely". The nearby Grammar School was founded in 1585 by Archbishop Sandys and is open to the public. There are fascinating relics of the school's long history on show. Its most famous pupil was William Wordsworth whose description of the church remains apt:*

> *"like a throned lady sending out*
> *A gracious look all over her domain".*

Skating on Derwentwater

In fairyland we revelled all the day,
    Clear glass of gold lay Derwentwater's flood,
    Far Glaramara mailed in silver stood.
And Skiddaw bright for ivory inlay
Shone purple clad with royalest array
    To see our kingly sport. How leapt the blood!
    As on from sunny bay to shadowy wood
We flashed above the mirrors steely grey.

But when the sun o'er Newlands sank to rest
    Enchantment in the valley seemed to grow,
      There, while the snows were flushed on fell and moor
      Loud rang the skates upon a lilac floor,
And burning upward thro' the lake's dark breast
    Fire gleamed with unimaginable glow.

    H.D. Rawnsley

Fountains, Meadows, Hills, and Groves

And O, ye Fountains, Meadows, Hills, and Groves,
Forebode not any severing of our loves!
Yet in my heart of hearts I feel your might;
I only have relinquished one delight
To live beneath your more habitual sway.
I love the Brooks which down their channels fret,
Even more than when I tripped lightly as they;
The innocent brightness of a new-born Day
    Is lovely yet;
The Clouds that gather round the setting sun
Do take a sober colouring from an eye
That hath kept watch o'er man's mortality;
Another race hath been, and other palms are won.
Thanks to the human heart by which we live,
Thanks to its tenderness, its joys, and fears,
To me the meanest flower that blows can give
Thoughts that do often lie too deep for tears.

    William Wordsworth *(from 'Intimations of Immortality')*

Rydal Mount Wordsworth's Home 1813-1850

Wordsworth Remembered

Raised are the dripping oars,
Silent the boat! the lake,
Lovely and soft as a dream,
Swims in the sheen of the moon.
The mountains stand at its head
Clear in the pure June-night,
But the valleys are flooded with haze.

Rydal and Fairfield are there;
In the shadow Wordsworth lies dead.
So it is, so it will be for aye.
Nature is fresh as of old,
Is lovely; a mortal is dead.

The spots which recall him survive,
For he lent a new life to these hills.
The Pillar still broods o'er the fields
Which border Ennerdale Lake,
And Egremont sleeps by the sea.
The gleam of The Evening Star
Twinkles on Grasmere no more,
But ruined and solemn and grey
The sheepfold of Michael survives;
And, far to the south, the heath
Still blows in the Quantock coombs,
By the favourite waters of Ruth.
These survive!–yet not without pain,
Pain and dejection to-night,
Can I feel that their poet is gone.

Matthew Arnold *(from 'The Youth of Nature')*

The River Eden

Eden! till now thy beauty had I viewed
By glimpses only, and confess with shame
That verse of mine, whate'er its varying mood,
Repeats but once the sound of thy sweet name:
Yet fetched from Paradise that honour came,
Rightfully borne; for Nature gives thee flowers
That have no rivals among British bowers;
And thy bold rocks are worthy of their fame.
Measuring thy course, fair Stream! at length I pay
To my life's neighbour dues of neighbourhood;
But I have traced thee on thy winding way
With pleasure sometimes by this thought restrained–
For things far off we toil, while many a good
Not sought, because too near, is never gained.

   William Wordsworth

A Shadow on Scafell

IN MEMORIAM PROF. A. MILNE MARSHALL, OF OWENS COLLEGE, MANCHESTER, WHO DIED BY A FALL FROM THE CRAGS ABOVE LORD'S RAKE ON SCAFELL, 31st DECEMBER, 1893.

Clear shines the heaven above our New Year's day,
   The sunlight gleams by Wastdale's desolate shore
   And steams o'er grassy Gavel, and the floor
Of Derwentwater glitters gold and gay.
But one great shadow lingering seems to stay
   Dark on Scafell, beneath its summit hoar–
   Shadow more deep than gloomy Mickledore,
Shadow no New Year's sun can charm away.

For he who climbed so many crags of fear,
   Sounded such deeps, such heights of knowledge won,
     But never over-passed our heights of love,
     Has vanished in a moment–gone to prove
Those peaks beyond our seeing–and we hear
   Far up the cleft a brave voice: 'Follow on.'

   H.D. Rawnsley

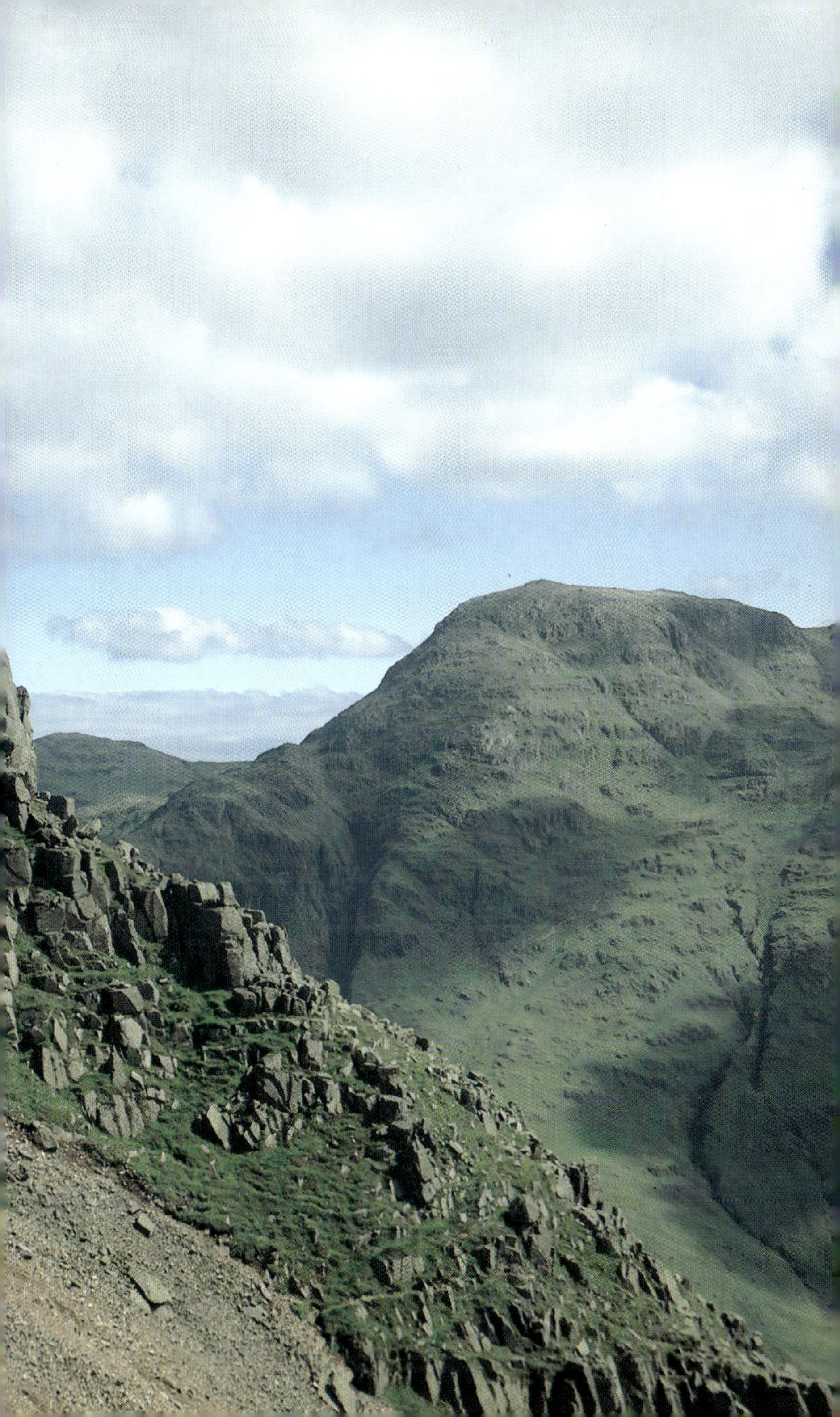

Index of Poets

ARNOLD, Matthew (1822-1888)
COLERIDGE, Hartley (1796-1849)
COLERIDGE, Samuel Taylor (1772-1834)
DALTON, John (1709-1763)
FABER, FW (1814-1863)
HEMANS, Felicia Dorothea (1793-1835)
KEATS, John (1795-1821)
NORTH, Christopher (1785-1854)
QUILLINAN, Edward (1791-1851)
RAWNSLEY, HD (1851-1920)
RUSKIN, John (1819-1900)
SCOTT, Walter (1771-1832)
SOUTHEY, Robert (1774-1843)
WORDSWORTH, William (1770-1850)

Index of First Lines

*denotes an extract from a longer poem

A barking sound the Shepherd hears	Wordsworth	60
And in the frosty season, when the sun	Wordsworth	72
A region desolate and wild*	Arnold	29
And O, Ye Fountains, Meadows, Hills, and Groves*	Wordsworth	74
As once I roam'd the fells, to brood	Quillinan	22
Beneath the full-orb'd moon, that bathed in light	North	65
Cheery Crosthwaite ringers	Rawnsley	9
Clear shines the heaven above our New Year's Day	Rawnsley	76
De Vaux had mark'd the sunbeams set*	Scott	42
Eden, till now thy beauty had I viewed	Wordsworth	76
God, for the gift of the thunder and fire I fear Thee	Rawnsley	70
Here, traveller, pause and think, and duly think	Coleridge	49
Horrors like these at first alarm*	Dalton	54
How does the water come down at Lodore	Southey	55
I climb'd the dark brow of mighty Helvellyn	Scott	58
I heard the wheat-ear singing in the dale	Rawnsley	12
I'll doubt no more that Fairies dwell*	Quillinan	25
In fairyland we revelled all the day	Rawnsley	74
In such a scene, on such a day	Quillinan	21
I saw a shepherd with a wounded lamb	Faber	23
Is this the lake, the cradle of the storms	North	17
I thought of Thee, my partner and my guide	Wordsworth	28
I've watched you now a full half hour	Wordsworth	70
I wandered lonely as a cloud	Wordsworth	14
I wandered lonely as a cloud	Wordsworth	15
I weary of the fountain foaming	Ruskin	31
Like a dismal cirque*	Keats	51
Low spirits are a sin, — a penance given	Faber	21
My heart leaps up when I behold	Wordsworth	64
Not a breath of air	Wordsworth	64
Not raised in nice proportions was the Pile	Wordsworth	11
Now lingers long the gold within the west	Rawnsley	67
O askest thou of me*	Faber	35
O Blithe new-comer! I have heard	Wordsworth	19

Once more I see thee, Skiddaw, once again	Southey	36
On stern Blencartha's perilous height	Coleridge, ST	53
On the verge of the hill we precariously stood*	Ruskin	47
O Reader! hast thou ever stood to see	Southey	12
O Vale and lake, within your mountain-urn	Hemans	33
Paled in by many a lofty hill*	Scott	41
Raised are the dripping oars*	Arnold	75
Rude is this Edifice, and Thou hast seen	Wordsworth	24
Shall I sing of little rills	Coleridge, H	34
The Cock is crowing	Wordsworth	14
The dark, narrow Thirlmere lay now at our feet*	Ruskin	52
The gentle Banks*	Wordsworth	68
The Kirk of Ulpha, to the pilgrim's eye	Wordsworth	28
There are no snow-white oxen in the dales	Rawnsley	23
There is a Lake hid far among the hills	North	17
There is a Yew Tree, pride of Lorton Vale	Wordsworth	11
There the sun himself*	Wordsworth	38
Up! up my friend, and quit your books	Wordsworth	37
We left, just ten years since, you say*	Arnold	48
We scaled, without a track to ease our steps*	Wordsworth	39
Where is the grave of Sir Arthur O'Kellyn	Coleridge, ST	53
Within the mind strong fancies work	Wordsworth	63